The Postures of Prayer

By Kimberly L. Ray

Dedication

I would like to dedicate this book to the Sainted memory of my late mother, Dr. Angie Ray. She was a Powerful Prayer Warrior and a compassionate minister of the Gospel; my first and greatest teacher who gave me a priceless, timeless treasure; a precious gift. She trained me from a child how to pray and reverence the presence of my Sovereign God. Only the heavens record the depth of my gratitude for her loving investment in my heart.

I honor God for my three natural sisters. Tanya, the baby girl, I am amazed by her Godly wisdom which is well beyond her years. I am convinced she was birthed into this world just for me.

Pastor J. Denise Ray is an absolute portrait of resilience and the essence of human compassion. She inspires me. Her matchless support is phenomenal and rare.

My sister Cheryl has shown the art of dedication, stick-to-itiveness, and tenacity in her work for the ministry. I am blessed beyond measure to have each of my treasured sisters in my life. My love for them is indescribable.

I honor the Lord for allowing me to be tremendously enriched and blessed by the life of my brother in Christ, the late Bishop Kervy Brown.

In life, God provides voices of wisdom. I extend my heartfelt thanks to Bishop Horace E. Smith, MD, Bishop I.V. Hilliard, Dr. Bill Winston, Pastor Billy Brewton, Bishop Michael Blue, and Bishop James Nelson, Sr. Your influence and insight have motivated me to continue on a path of intercession. You have all been strategic instruments in my life.

To my beautiful congregation, you all know that my love for you is exceedingly great.   I am also immensely grateful for all of my wonderful friends, especially my colleagues who are anointed intercessors.

Other Publications written by *Kimberly L. Ray*

The Heart Monitor

A 30-Day Spiritual Evaluation of the Heart. Each chapter and devotional enlighten the believer in the area of the heart through scripture.

Relentless Faith

How to utilize the faith described in the Word of God in your everyday life.

*Prevailing Prayers of the Bible

A compilation of Biblical prayers and the dialogue spoken to God by key vessels in the scripture.

Spiritual Intervention

Powerful Insights for Breakthrough Prayers. In Spiritual Intervention, it shows how to launch a successful prayer intercession especially during times of crisis. We can stage a spiritual intervention and bombard heaven on behalf of yourself and your loved ones.

Published by Charmisa House Publishing

Scripture quotations from KJV, NIV and NKJV versions of the Bible

Contents

Chapter 9

PRAYERS IN THE TEMPLE
"Let the church say amen"
ANNA

Chapter 10

LIFTING EYES IN PRAYER
"Father, I know that you always hear me"
JESUS

Chapter 11

LIFTING HOLY HANDS IN PRAYER
"Prayers without wrath or doubting"
PAUL THE APOSTLE

The Postures of Prayer

By Kimberly L. Ray

Preface

This book records the actual Biblical postures of prayer. I find this subject intriguing, captivating, and compelling because it tells the enthralling backstories of intense prayer, and also highlights the postures taken by iconic Biblical figures. Yes, they prayed, but this book will discuss the setting and significance of the postures assumed as they prayed to our Sovereign God.

NO, this is not just another ordinary book about the topic of prayer. This is a close observation of actions and actual biblical accounts of how prayer impacted the lives of famed, historic vessels.

I encourage you to integrate the prayerful dialogue found in scripture into your daily times of personal prayer. I pray that this book will be a powerful source and tool of motivation.

It is wonderful to talk to our Omnipotent and Omniscience God, knowing that He hears us and will answer our prayers. To date, I have not seen any other minister compile the specific postures of prayers recorded in the scriptures. I am humbled and grateful the Lord gave me this precious assignment to convey these critical, ancient details with Christians everywhere.

My soul has been incredibly blessed and eternally changed by my spiritual experiences relating to the presence of our Holy God. I have seen the outcome of the authentic power of Intercession, Deliverance and Healing. During my research of the Holy scriptures, I felt compelled to know more about the individuals in the Bible and their prayer relationship with Adonai, the name of God that is so sacred, that in some cultures, it cannot be spoken aloud.

I want to take you on a journey of discovery where men and women of God experienced divine guidance, answers, and instructions. As you read, you will notice during passionate, prayer dialogue various postures of prayer. For example, some were kneeling, bowing their heads in awe, while others were laying prostrate, thus experiencing the tremendous weight of the glory of the Lord. I urge you to carefully read the words of this book and apply the postures of prayer to your heart, mind, and soul. It is my prayer that you will be inspired.

"And Hannah answered and said, No, my lord, I am a woman of a sorrowful spirit: I have drunk neither wine nor strong drink, but have poured out my soul before the Lord."

-1st Samuel 1:15

CHAPTER 1

SILENT PRAYERS

"May we observe a moment of silence"

Hannah

And Hannah answered and said, No, my lord, I am a woman of a sorrowful spirit: I have drunk neither wine nor strong drink, but have poured out my soul before the Lord.
I Samuel 1:15

"*A*re you drunk?" Imagine the shock and stunning devastation of this question after spending time in intense, vehement silent prayer. She says, "No my Lord. I have poured out my soul before the Lord."

There is a captivating woman in the Old Testament named Hannah whose name means favor and grace. This woman's story stands out in Biblical history for wanting something so passionately from

God. She is described as a woman who prayed so fervently and wept bitterly, signifying a deep, intense sorrow. This type of weeping was profound. This silent language spoke directly from the intelligence of her soul. It is more than just shedding tears. This timeless narrative of silence in prayer spoke volumes. It gives insight into the intuitive nature of this animated woman who had a request of El Shama, the God who hears.

It involves pouring out one's heart in times of gut-wrenching, emotional heartache and distress. Also, weeping bitterly is a description of times of excessive and boundless emotional turmoil. In this Biblical chronicle, Hannah was weeping because she wanted a child from the Lord. Her soul longed for a child.

I would like to highlight this posture of prayer that includes something extraordinary. I invite you to focus your full attention on the emphasis here; it is about the power of Hannah's silent prayer. In this case, she displayed the complete absence of verbal sound, not an echo, not the slightest resonance of a sound reverberation, not the use or power of speech, yet, this did not stop God from hearing this passionate inaudible, ardent petition. Although she was silent, the Lord heard the intelligence of her heart. God was able to hear what she was unable to verbalize. This woman who was recorded in Biblical history, displays a life of vehement and fervent silent prayer. In this exceptional moment, Hannah has an intense encounter with the Lord.

During this period of time in scripture, she felt utterly dejected and emotionally distraught. As a result, her internal plea to God was heartfelt because she cried within herself desperately longing for her own son.

Hannah was married to a man named Elkanah. During the time of the culture, he had two wives; one named Hannah and the other wife's name was Peninnah. Peninnah's significance was celebrated by Elkanah because she had children, but Hannah was barren, unfruitful, and unable to conceive.

Every year, Elkanah and his two wives would journey to a city called "Shiloh" for the purpose of worshipping and sacrificing unto the Lord of hosts. The priest of the Lord, Eli, who earlier assumed that Hannah was drunk, and his two sons Hophni and Phinehas were also present. Elkanah genuinely loved his wife Hannah but the Lord had shut up her womb. Elkanah felt a paramount level of frustration because of his inability to make Hannah happy. Elkanah's desperation to give Hannah a son highlighted his obsequious attempt to please her, despite her infertility.

During this time in scripture, it was very important to have a child as it was a sign of fruitfulness and God's blessings. Peninnah would provoke Hannah over and over, consistently taunting her and making her fret because she was reminded that she had no children. This caused Hannah to be clothed in a garment of sadness; a tapestry woven with dissatisfaction, distress, and a psychological state of grief. Therefore, Hannah wept bitterly and refused to eat at times.

Elkanah said to her, "Hannah, why weepest thou? And why eatest thou not? And why is thy heart grieved? Am not I better to thee than ten sons?" I Samuel 1:8. Elkanah showed exasperation and helplessness in his effort to comfort Hannah.

During this time, Eli, the high priest, who's role was to administer justice, sat up on a throne-like seat by the post of the temple of the Lord. He was an eye witness and noticed that Hannah was reeling and weeping in utter bitterness of soul, sobbing, and crying constantly.

She was shedding tears and internally bewailing longing disappointment because she had no child. In her silent prayer within herself, Hannah vowed to the Lord and said, "Lord of hosts, look upon the affliction of thy handmaid, remember me and not forget. But, give unto thy handmaid a man child and I will give him unto you Lord all the days of his life and there shall no razor come upon his head." Hannah prayed this specific prayer in silence; a silence that abstained from all sound, speech, or verbal discussion. This was Hannah's way of pouring out her soul before the Lord in prayer. In absolute silence she shared her authentic truth.

This story gives indication that in moments when words are not adequate or sufficient to express the concerns of your soul, God will perceive every unspoken word. He knows. There are times in the life of a believer when your prayers will be internal and no words will be spoken verbally aloud, but God will discern the words of your heart without the use of a whisper, which is speaking softly without using your vocal cords, or a definitive cry. In this prayer, Hannah made a vow to God.

Please note, in Biblical times, an unshaved head was a sign of devoted consecration and separation unto God for His divine purpose alone. Hannah continued praying before the Lord. Hannah was speaking in her heart; only her lips moved but her voice was inaudible. Nevertheless, Hannah's posture of prayer was incredibly passionate.

I find it enthralling that Hannah's demonstrative behavior stood out to the Priest, so much so, that he assumed her exhibited gestures were signs of one who was drunken. In this moment, Eli, the high priest's surprisingly indiscernible perception speaks of his inability to discern or determine the actual state of Hannah's grief and complaint.

Hannah poured out her soul, thus speaking freely to God about her private and most deeply felt emotional pain. This pleading came from a crushed place of her soul's desire as she cried out desperately to God. Hannah was barren, yet preferred.

I thought of the fact that one who is drunk typically loses all control of their behavior and it is also said of a drunken person, that the core truth of whatever they are experiencing, thinking, enduring, or feeling internally will manifest. In Hannah's case, her words were not heard but her animated actions were indicative of her inner turmoil. In reality, Eli thought, as a matter of fact, that she was actually drunk.

Eli said to her, "Hannah, how long will thy be drunken? Put away thy wine from thee." Hannah answered and said, "No my lord! I am a woman of a sorrowful spirit. I have drunk neither wine nor strong drink but I have poured out my soul before the Lord." As a Christian you may discover that there are individuals you meet who may not be able to verbalize their personal plight or concerns. Note, at times, things are not always what they seem or appear to be.

As a ministry gift, or an intercessor, I urge you to pray that God will grant you keen discernment to perceive and differentiate between a person you are praying for who is unable to speak; to actually know the difference between drunkenness and a pain. I would like to encourage you as you reflect upon the story of Hannah to glean from her **posture of prayer** and similarly be as passionate in your prayer time. In those moments when you are unable to speak your prayer audibly, remember Hannah.

No matter how difficult the subject is during your personal prayer time, I implore you to share your authentic self; whatever is on the altar of your heart, tell the Lord the truth about it. As you pour out your soul, you release every burden of your mind, will, and emotions. As you are honest in His presence, you set a precedence of humility, which is the gateway to the presence of God. A broken and contrite spirit, the Lord will not despise. God will hear the cry of your soul. Even when others misinterpret the behavior, similarly to Eli the Priest, God knows the genuine state of your affairs. Tell God all that troubles you in prayer. Whatever it is, take it to the Lord in prayer.

During her conversation with Eli, Hannah said "count not thine handmaid for a wicked daughter of the enemy." She did not want anything to hinder her request; also, she wanted to separate herself from the category of the wicked daughters. She goes on in prayer to say "for out of the abundance of my complaint and grief, have I spoken until now." The priest Eli answered and said unto Hannah, "Go in peace and the God of Israel grant thee thou petition that thou hast asked of Him." In this moment, Eli the Priest confirmed to Hannah that the Lord had heard her prayer and would grant her request. Hannah replied to Eli, and said, "Let thy handmaid find grace in thy sight." "So, Hannah went her way and did eat and her countenance was no longer sad."

The next day, Hannah arose early in the morning, gratified, and enraptured in worship before the Lord. This is intoxication! A jubilant, cheerful disposition, with confidence knowing that God heard her soundless, silent prayer. She then returned to her house and the Lord remembered her prayer. Hannah was blessed by God to bear a son named Samuel. And Hannah said, "Because I have asked him of the Lord."

This triumphant testimony is evidence of the faithfulness of God.

After the birth of Samuel, Hannah brought the child to Eli and she said, "Oh my lord, as thy soul liveth, my lord, I am the woman that stood by thee here praying unto the Lord." In this moment, Hannah is reminding the Priest of the day that she prayed in silence and wept sorely and was mistaken for being drunk. She said to Eli, "For this is the child that I prayed for and the Lord hath given me my petition which I have asked of Him. Therefore also, I have lent him to the Lord. As long as he liveth, he shall be loaned to the Lord." Hannah's willingness to give Samuel over to serve in the temple is a beautiful characterization of love and obedience. "And Eli the priest worshipped there." Without fail, God heard the silent prayer of Hannah. What a triumphant victory.

It is beautiful to see how Hannah kept her vow to the Lord concerning her son Samuel. Samuel went on to become a faithful young servant who had God's favor; a Prophet of God who was chosen to take the horn of the anointing oil and anoint the prominent Kings of Israel which are Saul and David. He was instructed to take the horn of the anointing oil which contained a mixture of myrrh, cassia, calamus, olive oil, and cinnamon.

"And they fell upon their faces and the glory of the Lord appeared unto them."

-Numbers 20:6

Chapter 2

PROSTRATE PRAYERS

"Lay your face before God"

Moses & Aaron

And they fell upon their faces and the glory of the Lord appeared unto them.

Numbers 20:6

I want to share with you, years ago as a young pastor, specifically after the death of my late mother, a precious church mother named Rachel Sellers gave me commanding yet enlightening words of wisdom from her years of experience. She said, "Kimberly, I want to share some things with you." She said emphatically, "I want to encourage you as a young Pastor to take the people to the Lord in prayer." She said, "Kimberly, you must lay your face before God!" Which in essence means to give yourself wholly to a life of fasting and prayer for this pastoral assignment.

Mother Sellers encouraged me to take the people of God into His Presence. She said, "You are going to have to deal with people and you've got to forgive quickly!" She went on to say, "Do not let it get in your heart!" This mother in Zion was preparing me to face some of the unrelenting uncertainties of life. She wanted me to avoid any bitterness, anger, vitriol, or anything that would block my prayers in the future.

I would like to echo the words of this anointed prayer warrior…Whatever happens in your life, forgive quickly, and release it.

What does forgiveness mean? It means, "I release you from the punishment I feel you deserve because of what you've done to me." One of the reasons why it is so important to forgive is that you don't want anything to hinder your prayers or to grieve the heart of God when you go before Him in prayer.

I was struck by another instance of an elder statesmen; a Bishop from the city of Jamaica Queens New York; a mighty man of God. He was the honorable Bishop John Boyd, Sr. He was a highly respected consecrated vessel of God known for his dynamic prayer ministry.

On one particular occasion, I was invited to speak at his church service, at Bethel in New York. This invitation was overwhelming and a high honor because of the Godly reputation of Bishop Boyd. I had the honor of meeting the Bishop before we went into the sanctuary. I was escorted up a long stair case to his office. This awesome, powerful man of God was wearing a pure white three-piece suit with a crisp French white shirt, white tie and sharp white shoes. There was something unique about this praying Bishop that I will never forget as long as

I shall live. Right before service, he suggested that we have a word of prayer before going down to the sanctuary.

As we stood, Bishop felt led to pray. In this moment, he got on his knees and laid out prostrate on the floor. He stretched out and began calling on the Lord, while on his face. I had never seen or experienced an awe and an anointing that completely overwhelmed my soul during the prayer. I felt the weight of the presence of Almighty God that day. It caused a type of reverential fear to come upon me in that moment.

This is a fond example of the first time I ever witnessed the strength and humility of the posture of a prostrate prayer. I was silenced within with a sense of reverence and clarity of the voice of the Lord in preparation to minister the word of God for that service. One of Bishop Boyd's sayings that touched my life was "God can do more in five minutes of prayer, than you can do on your own in a lifetime." He was irreplaceable.

In the book of Numbers, Moses was chosen to be the deliverer of the children of Israel. He is confronted with a group of people who were upset with him because they did not have water. They were thirsty and angry, accusing Moses of bringing them into the wilderness to die. They were hostile, saying, "Why did you bring the congregation of the Lord up out of Egypt to bring us to this evil place." They angrily said, "There are no seeds, vines, pomegranates or water to drink."

Let me establish that the people were furious with Moses even after all of the miracles they had witnessed and experienced.

Now let us observe what Moses and Aaron did during this crisis. "They went from the presence of the assembly unto the door of the tabernacle of the congregation, and they fell upon their faces; and the glory of the Lord appeared unto them." This **posture of prayer** really stood out to me because Moses did not become combative or defensive with the people. He responded by turning his focus to God in a crisis moment when help was needed. He chose to bow himself to the earth, lay on his face in prayer before the Lord. This **posture of prayer** signifies a total dependence upon God and Moses' willingness to humbly go to God for answers.

The primary Hebrew word for worship Is "Shachah" which means "to bow down or prostrate oneself in homage." It is after Moses and Aaron laid before the Lord, then the glory fell.

The glory of the Lord refers to the visible manifestation of the presence of God. It is the weighty majestic presence, power, and the very splendor of God. It is described as divine light, grandeur, beauty, and spiritual transcendence; the visible man And the Lord spake to Moses and told him to take the rod, gather the assembly and Aaron. He was instructed to speak to the rock before their eyes; and it shall give forth it's water, and thou shalt bring forth to them water out of the rock; so thou shalt give the congregation and their beasts drink."

Apparently, Moses lifted his hands, and with his rod he smote the rock twice: the water came out abundantly and the congregation drank hearty manner, and their beasts also.

It is my hope that the posture of praying prostrate will come to mind in your life when you are faced with a critical place that requires you to be decisive. I hope you remember to utilize this posture as an option during your time of prayer. I believe that God will honor the act of submissive humility.

As an intercessor, strive to spend more time laying prostrate before Him like in ancient times. In those times, when you don't know the way and when you don't see the way, you must learn how to trust Him. I encourage you to learn how to lean on Him and say, "God, I don't know the way. But You know. So, I trust You. I'm going to trust You with my life, knowing that your word declares that you have a good plan for me; a plan for good and not evil. I'm going to trust You with my future, knowing the steps of a good man are ordered by the Lord. It is my prayer for you that you walk and follow after the path of God.

"Then went king David in, and sat before the Lord."

-2nd Samuel 7:18

CHAPTER 3

SITTING PRAYERS

"You may be seated"

DAVID

Then went king David in, and sat before the Lord. 2 Samuel 7:18

"*Y*ou may be seated." It is a general phrase often used in the Christan church by officiants, ministers, or designated leaders who formally and politely instruct everyone in unison the permission to be seated in the church. This practice helps to manage the transitions of the service, keeping the congregation focused and in order. In this chapter, we will explore an amazing Biblical posture of prayer that is sure to be a blessing in your life.

Arguably, David is one of the most prominent figures in the word of God, known for his bravery, leadership, mercy, and repentance. He was considered one of Israel's greatest Kings. It is a joy for me to write about King David. He is one of my favorite Biblical vessels. A King, a Shepherd, a Warrior, a chief musician, a giant slayer, and one who is noted as being a man after God's own heart. The youngest son of Jesse, who's life from his youth to his old age is one of the most intriguing and riveting stories of the Bible.

I observed in the book of 2nd Samuel 7, a **posture of prayer**. This story begins with David talking to the Lord. In this instance, God tells David that he is giving him a season of rest from war and from his enemies.

In this account, Nathan, the prophet is giving positive instructions to David. Nathan told David to go and do all that is thy heart for the Lord is with thee. In this passage, Almighty God is encouraging David after many battles, a season of attacks, and a long period of war. The Lord said that He was with David wherever he went and has cut off all of his enemies in his sight. The Lord reminds David that He has made his name great among all of the men who are in the earth. The Lord allowed David to survive as a valiant warrior and be ruler over many people. The Lord spoke regarding the people of Israel and He said, "I will plant them and they shall dwell within a place of their own and move no more." God is so mindful, He says to David, "I am giving thee rest from all thine enemies. I will establish my kingdom."

Note, in this **posture of prayer**, King David sat before the Lord as God instructed Him. *You may be seated.* This was in instruction given by God, a type of permission to take time to rest. I say to everyone reading this book that each of us are granted a time of rest from labor and war. While seated, he began to talk to God in a moment where he felt unworthy but grateful considering the mighty work of God and how God granted him a season of rest. David sat down in a place where he could be fully invested in the presence of the Lord. The act of being seated before the Lord symbolizes a posture of introspection, contemplation, reflection, and prayer. It is also a place of personal communion and fellowship with God, the Father.

He began to tell God in prayer, "Who am I, Sovereign Lord, and what is my family, that you have brought me this far?" David is talking to the Lord from a place of humility and overwhelmed by God's great plans for he and his family. During sitting prayers, I would like to encourage you to remember the faithfulness of God and to glean from the posture of David as he shares heartfelt sentiments of gratefulness unto God. I love how David talks to God and speaks of Him as being an awesome wonder.

Understandably, much of this commentary is centered around David's seated posture. I love the fact that David is sitting in this instance as he is extolling God and telling him, "God, there is none like thee, neither is there any God beside thee." He was reminding God "How great you are, Sovereign Lord! There is no one like you, and there is no God but you, as we have heard with our own ears.

It goes on to say in 2nd Samuel 7:23, "And who is like your people Israel—the one nation on earth that God went out to redeem as a people for himself, and to make a name for himself, and to perform great and awesome wonders by driving out nations and their gods from before your people, whom you have redeemed from Egypt." David proclaims to God "You have established your people Israel as your very own forever, and you, Lord, have become their God."

It is magnificent to me how David magnified God. He said, "The Lord of hosts is the God is Israel." In Biblical times, the Lord of Hosts was described as the God whose emphasis is upon His Sovereignty and power over all creation, including the heavenly armies and Angelic beings. This description celebrates God as Chief ruler and Command of all Celestial beings and earthly powers. I love how the Bible describes in the New Testament book of Hebrews 4:9 similar words that were spoken to David. It further communicates the message that there remains therefore a rest for the people of God.

In the life of every believer, prayer warrior, or prayer advocate, I say to you that there is a season of rest that God will provide for you. This includes warfare, dealing with spiritual attacks, and as in the case of David, from being on the run from the enemy.

I can imagine the relief and peace David must have felt as he understood that the God that taught His hands to war and his fingers to fight is now giving him rest from his enemies. I say to you, hear this message. God has promised us rest. This mandate speaks of a state of resting after exertion or strain. I lose upon you rest: physically, mentally, psychologically. I encourage you to stop right now, take a deep breath, and rest! Like David, "you may be seated."

"Joy is an outflow of an indwelling peace and assurance that exists during prayer."

"I love to pray surrounded by nature. We close our eyes in prayer considering that some of the most beautiful things in life are not always seen but felt especially within the heart."

-Kimberly L. Ray

"And the man bowed down his head."

-Genesis 24:26

CHAPTER 4

BOWING PRAYERS

"May we bow our heads in prayer"

The Servant of Abraham

And the man bowed down his head.
Genesis 24:26

I would like to begin by sharing with you a **Posture of Prayer** that is incredibly important. For many years, we have heard the words "May we bow our heads in prayer" during our Sunday worship services. I would like to share with you an actual account discovered in the Holy Bible that references bowing one's head in prayer.

In the Pentateuch, which is the first five books of law in the Old Testament, the book of Genesis records the story of Abraham. In this account, he was described as very old and well stricken in age. In spite of this, the Lord blessed Abraham in all things. It is remarkable to note that he had the high honor of being called a friend of God. His friendship with God is referenced in the Book of Isaiah chapter 41:8.

I believe it is important to emphasize that Abraham, the father of many nations, moved God by his remarkable faith and his life of mutual trust and dependency upon God. Abraham's love for God caused him to look to Him for guidance. He walked before Him in a way that developed and formed this remarkable friendship with God. I find it amazing that of all of the men recorded in the Bible, Abraham was referenced as having a bond of fellowship with God that gave him the distinct honor of being called a friend of God.

Abraham proved His love for God through his acts of obedience to the voice of God. Abraham was blessed to have a son at the age of 100 years old. As we review the story of Abraham, I would like to share a specific instance that is connected to the son whom he loved. Abraham had a son named Isaac in his old age. When Isaac was of age for marriage, this is what unfolded. In my opinion, I considered this as one of the most beautiful stories I have read concerning blessings for one's faithfulness.

In a conversation, Abraham said unto the eldest servant of his house, "Put, I pray thee, thy right hand under my thigh and swear by the Lord, the God of Heaven and the God of the earth, **that you will not** take a wife unto my son of the daughters of the Canaanites among whom I dwell." Abraham gave a passionate request because he wanted his son to marry someone of his kindred. He asked the servant to "go unto my country and my kindred and take a wife unto my son Isaac." And the servant of

Abraham said unto him, "Perhaps the woman will not be willing to follow me unto this land. And the servant of Abraham inquired of him, "Should I bring your son to the land where you are from?"

Let us review Abraham's immediate and swift response. He said to him, "No, I do not want you to bring my son here again." Abraham wanted to convey to his servant that the Lord God of heaven who took Him from his father's house, the land of his kindred and spoke unto him saying "thy seed will I give this land." During this discussion with God, Abraham had an assurance because God had spoken to him. The Lord revealed that he would "send angels before thee and thou shalt take a wife unto my son from thence."

In essence, here is the confirmation of the surety and certainty of a vessel who embraces the words from God to his servant Abraham. God promised him that He would send the Angels before him and his son would have a wife from his country. In the midst of this conversation, Abraham states to his servant, "if the woman is not willing to follow thee, then thou shalt be clear from this my oath."

In an act of trust, servitude, and obedience, the servant placed his hand under the thigh of Abraham his master, which was a sign that the servant agreed to carrying out his special request.

The servant of Abraham took ten camels of his master and departed to a city called Nahor. The servant caused the 10 camels to kneel outside of the city by a well of water. In Biblical times, the water of a well was significant. Almost every aspect of daily life in Ancient Israel involved the need for water. Young women typically had the daily chore of drawing water from wells to supply the family household. The women would lower the vessel into the well to collect the water and then carry the vessel. The well was also considered a gathering place for travelers to stop and water their camels. In some instances, the wells were considered landmarks.

It stands out to me that the servant had a heart of prayer during his assigned mission from Abraham to locate a wife for Isaac. In prayer, the servant said, "O Lord God of my master Abraham, please give me success this day, and show kindness to my master Abraham."

This part of the story is fascinating. Here the loyal servant of Abraham stands by a well of water as the women of the town came to draw water. Not only did Abraham have a rapport with God in prayer as His friend but, his servant showed a continual sensitivity and reverence to God in his communication during prayer as well. In this moment,

The Servant prays, "And let it come to pass, that the damsel to whom I shall say, Let down thy pitcher, I pray thee, that I may drink; and she shall say, Drink, and I will give thy camels drink also: let the same be she that thou hast appointed for thy servant Isaac; and thereby shall I know that thou hast shewed kindness unto my master." Genesis 24:14

Imagine experiencing a long, grueling journey with 10 resilient camels who represent adaptability in dry, sweltering, and desert-like conditions, having traveled from a far country. I am sure the need for water was extremely great. And the Bible says "and it came to pass before he had done speaking with his servant, Rebekah came with her pitcher upon her shoulder." The Bible describes Rebekah as being very beautiful to look upon. The scripture also indicates that she was a virgin.

In this lovely story, the timing of God is wonderful. We observe that Rebekah came to the well, filled her pitcher, and the servant of Abraham ran to meet her and said, "Let me, I pray thee, drink a little water from thy pitcher." In this moment, the servant is searching to see if the fulfillment of his prayer was unfolding. In his heart, he prayed that the girl that he was searching for, on behalf of his master, would be the one offering water to him and his camels. Rebekah said, "drink my Lord" and she hasted and let down her pitcher and gave him drink. And when she had completed giving him water, would you believe she asked the question that the servant was waiting to hear?

Rebekah confirmed that God was orchestrating her steps and unveiling His perfect will. Just as the servant prayed, it is Rebekah who initiated the request saying, "I will draw water for thy camels also until they have done drinking" and she hasted and emptied her pitcher and ran again unto the well to draw water for the 10 camels. And the servant of Abraham said, "Whose daughter are you?" Rebekah confirmed in this moment that she was kin to Abraham; this serves as further manifestation and confirmation of the will of God. Rebekah offered hospitality and lodging to the servant. She said "we have straw and enough feed and room for you to stay."

Let us witness this powerful posture of the servant of Abraham. In a moment of satisfied gratitude unto God, here is the **posture of prayer. "And the man bowed down his head."** Bowing one's head is a sign of reverence, respect, and humility, particularly during moments of reflection.

This demonstration of bowing the head was a powerful gesture indicative of a moment of reverence and respect for the presence of God. Even today this

posture of prayer is practiced all over the world. Many churches everywhere begin their prayer by saying to the congregation, "Let us bow our heads in prayer." I would further like to mention the reason we close our eyes in prayer is to reverence God and to minimize distractions. For many, prayer is a private matter between a person and God. Closing your eyes is a way to block out distractions and focus your attention on the conversation with God. Closing your eyes also helps to turn your thoughts internally. During prayer, this is an appropriate way to show humility.

This posture also indicates that the Servant of Abraham knew that God was orchestrating his steps by leading and guiding him to Rebekah. Again, this posture of bowing one's head before the Lord is important. It is also a silent acknowledgement of God's holy presence and our dependence on His intervention.

Can you imagine the sight of this beautiful, young, fair damsel Rebekah in a far country who was not only willing to offer water for the servant and his camels but suggested lodging also. While worshipping the Lord, the servant began to pray this prayer. He blessed the God of his master Abraham and honored God for not leaving him destitute in a far country, but rather showed him mercy, truth, and kindness. He took time to honor God for leading him to the house of his master's brethren.

Abraham's servant revealed to Rebekah's family that he had come on behalf of his master, Abraham. He told them that the Lord had blessed his master greatly. He wanted to convey to them that his master had become great. With bold confidence, he assured the family that God had given his master flocks, herds, menservants, maidservants, and camels. He also mentioned "My master's wife Sarah bore a son when she was 90 years old. My master, Abraham made me swear that I would not take a daughter of the Canaanites. And Abraham said unto me, The Lord, before whom I walk, will send his angel with thee, and prosper thy way; and thou shalt take a wife for my son of my kindred, and of my father's house: And **"I bowed down my head and I worshiped the Lord."**

Rebekah's family agreed that this thing proceeded from the Lord. They felt clarity and assurance that this was God. And they said, "Rebekah is before thee, take thee and go and let her be thy master's son's wife as the lord has spoken." And it came to pass, that when Abraham's servant heard their words, **"he bowed himself to the earth."**

The act of bowing to the earth was another posture of prayer and sign of gracious gratitude. It marked the servant's peace and submission to God's will. It is also clear that the servant of Abraham had a heart full of appreciation. Bowing to the earth was respectful acknowledgment for the way he was received by Rebekah's family in a far country.

"And her father and brother called Rebekah and said unto her, 'will thou go with this man?' And she said, "I will go." And they sent Rebekah and her nurse with Abraham's servant and his men. Although her mother wanted her to stay an additional 10 days, Rebekah's family blessed her and said "thou are our sister, be thou the mother of thousands, of millions, and let thy seed possess the cities of their enemies." The family agreed that this was the divine will of God.

Let us observe how Abraham's son, Isaac, responded, as he was meditating in the field as he lifted up his eyes and saw the camels coming and his future wife Rebekah walking towards him.

I am delighted at this story of blossoming love and how Rebekah lifted and quickly dismounted from her camel when she saw Isaac. Imagine her joy as she asked this question "who is this man that walketh in the field to meet us?" Abraham's faithful servant confirmed to her, 'It is my master!' For the first time, Rebekah met Isaac. Isaac was pleased and brought her to his mother Sarah's tent, and she became his wife, and he loved her profoundly and was comforted after the death of his mother, Sarah.

"And Solomon stood before the altar of the Lord: and spread forth his hands toward heaven."

-1 Kings 8:22

Chapter 5

PRAYERS WITH HANDS SPREAD FORTH

"At the altar with hands spread forth to heaven"

Solomon

And Solomon stood before the altar of the Lord: and spread forth his hands toward heaven. 1 Kings 8:22

*I*n 1994, I was blessed with an all-expense paid trip to tour Israel. During my time there, I was invited to go to the wailing wall. I was given an instruction to place a prayer request on a small piece of paper. I remember folding the paper several times to ensure that it would fit into the tiny crevice of the wall. To this very day, that prayer request remains. The Western wall in the old city of Jerusalem is a place considered sacred and a location for the Pilgrimage of precious Jewish people. The wailing wall is considered uniquely Holy and is known as a fragment called "Solomon's Wall." Considered a place of weeping, many stand before the wall with devotions with the belief that God said that His divine presence would never depart from the wailing wall.

I would like to point your attention to another posture of prayer. In the book of 1 Kings 8:22, the Bible says, "And Solomon stood before the altar of the LORD in the presence of all the congregation of Israel, and spread forth his hands toward heaven." I want you to make note of this posture of lifting the hands toward heaven. This is important because it shows how Solomon prayed at times.

Solomon was noted in the scripture for his remarkable wisdom. He was granted a discerning heart to govern and direct God's people. He was the son born to

David and Bathsheba; the LORD allowed him to ask a specific request of God. Of the many things that he could have requested, he asked God for wisdom. The Bible says that Solomon, when he stood before God, he came to the altar with his hands spread forth to heaven. Standing reflects being ready to receive from God. I want you to add this story to your spiritual arsenal today. Take this posture of prayer: "I'm going to stand like Solomon, and lift my hands in prayer."

Solomon assembled the elders of Israel, the heads of the tribes, and the chief of the fathers of children of Israel for the purpose of bringing the ark of the covenant of the Lord out of the city of David, which is Zion. All the elders took up the ark and all of the holy vessels did the priests and the Levites bring. King Solomon sacrificed before the Lord and the priest brought the ark of the covenant into the house, the most Holy place. The ark contained the two tables of stone. And it came to pass, when the priests came out of the holy place, the glory of the Lord was so prevalent that it filled the house and the priests could not stand to minister because of the cloud. Then Solomon said, the Lord said "here I will dwell. I have surely built thee a house to dwell in." Imagine Solomon standing in a place where the presence of God would dwell for centuries and is considered sacred and Holy even until this very day.

Although his father David wanted to build the house of God, the Lord chose Solomon to build a house unto the Lord. God gave Solomon the task. And Solomon blessed all of the congregation of Israel and they stood. And he said, "he has built the house of the Lord where the ark is," wherein is the covenant. Embrace this posture during your time of prayer.

Solomon stood before the altar of the Lord in the presence of all the congregation of Israel, and spread forth his hand toward heaven and he prayed, "Lord God of Israel, there is no God like thee, in heaven above, or earth beneath, who keeps the covenant and mercy with thy servants that walk before thee with all their heart."

Solomon goes on to say "thou has fulfilled the request of my father, David. Lord, let thy word be verified which you spoke unto my father. Thank you for hearkening to the cry and the supplication of thy servant.

Note, a supplication is a humble request addressed to God, seeking guidance, mercy, and assistance. This form of prayer is a petition where one expresses their needs or desires to God with reverence and humility.

Solomon states, "Lord, when thou hearest our prayers, forgive any trespasses, condemn any wickedness, and judge the righteous. Forgive the sin of thy people, teach your people the good way in which they should walk. For anyone that spreads their hands towards this place, hear thou in heaven thou dwelling place for thou, only thou, knowest the heart." I realized and determined within myself to observe Solomon as he was asking God to remember the circumstances and prayers of any man who was lifting their hands toward the temple to pray that they may fear Him all of the days that they dwell in the land that God has given. Solomon is praying that others will hear of God's great name, strong hand, and stretched out arm that all people may fear thee and that the house is called by thy name.

Unwilling to take any credit for himself, Solomon prays saying, "Lord, these are your people, thine inheritance which you bought out of Egypt and from the midst of the furnace of iron." Solomon began his prayer standing, with his hands lifted, but before the prayer was concluded, the Bible says that he arose from the altar of the Lord from kneeling on his knees with his hands spread to heaven. After praying, he stood and blessed all of the congregation of Israel with a loud voice saying, "Not one word of all of his good promises will fail. The Lord our God be with us, He won't leave us, nor forsake us that all of the people of the earth may know that the Lord is God.

After praying with his hands lifted to God, honoring God for the sacrifices, Solomon sent the people away. They were joyful and glad of heart for all of the goodness the Lord had done.

"Then fell I down upon my face, and cried with a loud voice, and said, Ah Lord God! wilt thou make a full end of the remnant of Israel?"

-Ezekiel 11:13

Chapter 6

WEEPING PRAYERS
"Lord, will you destroy the remnant?"
Ezekiel

Then fell I down upon my face, and cried with a loud voice, and said, Ah Lord God! wilt thou make a full end of the remnant of Israel? **Ezekiel 11:13**

*H*ave you ever observed the state of the nations? The trouble, tyranny, and wickedness of mankind? Have you ever seen the judgment of God on display? Have you ever been shaken to a place of weeping because of the state of the church and God's people? Let us take a close look at a posture that caused the prophet to weep.

Whenever I think of Ezekiel, his name evokes emotions that cause you to want to understand his plight. Ezekiel is the author of the Old Testament book that bears his name. His name means "strengthened by God." He grew up in Jerusalem and was trained to be a priest in the temple. Ezekiel was used as a mouth piece to prophesy to God's people. He was active as a Prophet in the kingdom of Judah and sadly, he prophesied the impending destruction of Judah's capital city, Jerusalem.

A real prophet of God does not only prophesy good things and a rosy future. Similarly to Jeremiah's cry, "Oh that my head were waters and my eyes a fountain of tears that I may weep for the slain of the daughters of my people," in Ezekiel's case, he was commissioned by God to warn the people of God's impending judgment. The judgement of God denotes a process of consequences resulting from wicked behavior. God called Ezekiel to prophesy which is the communication of a divine message directly from God foretelling future events delivering guidance or unforeseen warnings. Prophets are seen as intermediaries between God and man.

In this sobering chapter, let us take note of what actually caused the judgment of God and the people of Israel. The Lord spoke to Ezekiel to prophesy about a man named Pelatiah who was one of the two princes whom the Lord showed Ezekiel. The Lord said, "Son of man, these are the men who devise mischief and give wicked counsel in this city, therefore prophesy against them, oh son of man." In the text, Pelatiah was guilty of giving wicked counsel during the Babylonian siege of Jerusalem. He was corrupt and had a disreputable character.

Here's what's important, Pelatiah was the son of the famed Benaiah, who's name means "the Lord has built." Benaiah was one of King David's loyal, high-ranking, mighty men of his military troops and he was noted for his valiant bravery. I want to mention that the Bible describes Pelatiah's father Benaniah as a heroic and audacious warrior who was noted for his spirited exploits. He was a courageous fighter who famously went down into a pit on a snowy day and killed a lion. In one case, Benaiah struck down a huge Egyptian. Although the Egyptian had a spear in his hand, Benaiah went against him with a club. He later snatched the spear from the Egyptian's hand and killed him with his own spear. Benaiah, son of Jehoida, was one of the famous three mighty warriors of David. He later became a commander in the army.

In this passage in the book of Ezekiel chapter 11, Ezekiel saw a vision from God during the time of Babylonian exile. Ezekiel was troubled by the wickedness that God revealed unto him. In this case, Ezekiel began to warn the people of Israel and tell them that they would know that God is Lord. It was a message of judgment from God that He would judge them in the border of Israel and that they should know that He is the Lord. His bold declaration spoke of their wickedness and unwillingness to walk in His statutes. The judgement of God was going to fall because they did not follow after the manner that was instructed but rather adopted the ways of the heathen. Ezekiel prophesied and while he spoke prophetically, Pelatiah fell dead.

Of all the **postures of prayer** highlighted in this book, it was something outstanding about this posture that struck me. I noticed how the scripture says that Ezekiel fell down upon his face. We have established that lying on one's face is the ultimate sign of submission. He cried vehemently weeping with a loud, thunderous voice and said "Ah, Lord God! Will thou destroy all of the remnant of Israel?" Ezekiel questioned if God would destroy all that remained from a godly period of time like in Jehoida's day.

I would like to express this truth; there are times when God will allow a weeping prayer to emerge in your spirit because of the sins of a nation. In the case of Ezekiel, he wept because of the judgement of God. The **posture of prayer**, weeping described the heartache the prophet experienced because of God's sore displeasure. In Biblical times, weeping refers to crying tears that signify a plethora of human emotions such as sorrow, grief, and yes, even repentance. When a prophet of God understood the pulse of the heart of God, they wept as a symbol of deep, emotional response to significant events described in the scripture.

I want to speak of one of Ezekiel's dilemmas. He watched God execute his judgment because of the wicked. His compelling cry, as he fell on his face weeping, was his way of expressing to God his struggle to see the end of a righteous remnant of Israel. The prophet Ezekiel groaned and moaned with a broken heart with bitter grief resulting from the judgment of God. His assignment was to warn the people.

I had an experience once at one of our international, intercessory prayer conferences. It was on a Saturday night, I was assigned to minister "live" on our international telecast "A Time of Intercession". I experienced something I had never felt before. The power of God fell upon me and I began to weep vehemently in the Spirit. I had never experienced a cry like this in my life.

Truthfully, I did not understand what I was feeling or hearing. The Lord gave me these words as I sought Him about this wailing and weeping that came up out of my soul. I heard these words in the realm of the spirit "An ominous cloud."

I had absolutely, positively no idea what these words meant. It was not long after this experience that the coronavirus descended upon our world. The outbreak of coronavirus disease (COVID-19) infected millions of people. This respiratory illness caused the death of countless. I believe that God was revealing to me the impending crisis that came in the form of a disease. All I know is that I saw a slow-moving dark cloud that I did not understand. 1st Corinthians 13:9 says, "For we know in part and we prophesy in part."

I am so glad that I was able to share with those who were close to me that I kept hearing these daunting words so that when this outbreak happened, others were able to see and help me understand that it was God speaking to me. I am not a person that overuses the term "The Lord told me or the Lord showed me." I have a fear and regard with great respect the presence of God. I am very cautious to say that He said something unless I have clarity that He is speaking to me. I will not say it unless I am sure that the Lord is speaking to me.

If you are a prayer warrior, I would like to encourage you to be sensitive to the move of the Holy Spirit when you are overtaken with a deep cry, lament, or a sense of wailing in the spirit. Know that God is revealing something to you that may be reflective of some trouble that will happen in the world.

I would like to say to any person who has a prophetic gift to understand the weight of your words. If you are called to prophesy, saying "Thus saith the Lord God," I pray that your message will be pure and a clear word from God. Know this, that every prophesy is not always pleasant. One thing I noticed about Ezkiel's time is that he cried out to God and God showed mercy. The Lord told Ezekiel, after the prophecies of judgment, that "I will gather your people and I will give you the land of Israel." It was clear that God wanted the people to take away all detestable and abominable things. After the repentance, He promised to put a new spirit within them and take out their stony hearts and give them a heart of flesh. God granted mercy unto to the people and brought restoration. Ezekiel plays a critical role as a comforter and consoler to God's people.

I pray that this chapter will help you understand moments in prayer when you feel an inexplicably deep cry and weep for our world, our nations, our cities, and for those who are in authority. Sometimes, you may experience this cry that will be a passionate cry for the state of the church and God's people. The Bible says in Proverbs 29:2, "when the righteous are in authority, the people rejoice: but when the wicked beareth rule, the people mourn." Similar to

Jeremiah, known as the weeping prophet, he too wept because of the state of a crumbling nation. God responds to the prayers of repentance. Jeremiah's lasting legacy is one of hope. Jeremiah 29:11 has offered expectation to believers for centuries. *For I know the thoughts that I think toward you, saith the Lord, thoughts of peace, and not of evil, to give you an expected end.*

"He kneeled upon his knees three times a day, and prayed"

-Daniel 6:10

Chapter 7

KNEELING PRAYERS
"While you're on your knees praying, God sends an angel"
DANIEL
"He kneeled upon his knees three times a day, and prayed" Daniel 6:10

One of my greatest memories as a young child was attending our weekly "live" radio broadcast. It aired on Sunday nights at 7:00 pm at our home church, The Monument of Faith. The late honorable Apostle Richard D. Henton would offer a life-changing, soul-stirring sermon. Just before he would begin his message, the mass choir, often in beautiful royal blue robes, would proclaim together a song led by the church's song leader at the time. His name was Claude Timmons. It became the anthem of the church entitled "Christ is the answer." The unforgettable lyrics began with these words "While you're on your knee praying, God sends and Angel and puts him on the run. And by the time you finish praying, that thing you have been praying for is already done. Christ is the answer."

Weekly this song prepared and charged the atmosphere for the preached word of God. As I wrote this chapter, the lyrics resounded in my mind as I share this **posture of prayer** recorded in the book of Daniel. I pray that it will speak to you in a prolific way.

Daniel was a prominent figure in the Bible. He was noted for being a noble young man. He was preferred by the president and princes because an excellent spirit was in him. He had profound wisdom and unwavering faith in God. Daniel's enemies assembled and went to King Darius. They asked the king to establish a statue and make a firm decree that whomsoever shall ask a petition of any God or man for 30 days except the king shall be cast into a den of lions! King Darius signed the writing and the decree.

The Bible states *"Now when Daniel knew that the writing was signed, he went down into his house; and his windows being open in his chamber toward Jerusalem, he kneeled upon his knees three times a day, and prayed, and gave thanks before his God, as he did aforetime."* Daniel 6:10

Kneeling during prayer is one of the most common postures of prayer. It reminds us of the spiritual demonstration of genuine humility. *Humility is a modest or low view of one's own importance.* Kneeling signifies reverence and submission to God. God is Sovereign. He is Almighty God. Yahweh is His name. Kneeling shows the importance of dependency on Him and how crucial it is to look to God, our Heavenly Father in prayer.

I want to share with you that kneeling before God indicates a willingness to place yourself in a posture of Godly submission. When you kneel before God, you are kneeling with intention. You are kneeling with the purpose of seeking the face of God for direction and answers.

The counselors, princes, and captains came together and as they assembled, they found Daniel praying and making supplications unto God. They went back to the king asking, "Haven't you signed a decree that no one should petition God or man for 30 days except you? Aren't they supposed to be casted into a den of lions?" The king responded, "Yes." The men said to the king, "Daniel does not regard your decree but he continues to make his petition three times a day." When the king heard these words, he was displeased within himself and set his heart on Daniel and how he could help him. The king agonized about this decision until the sun went down.

It is critical to observe the reality that Daniel's consequence for praying three times a day was that he was cast into den of lions. The king was so distraught that he passed the night fasting. He did not want to hear music and he could not sleep. The reason why the king agonized all night long was because God had given Daniel favor.

I am thrilled by this riveting part of the story. The king arose very early in the morning and made haste to the den of lions; when he came to the den, he cried with a loud, lamentable voice unto Daniel. He said, "O, Daniel, servant of the living God, is thy God whom thou servest continually able to deliver thee from the lions?"

Can you imagine the king feeling terrified and tormented at the thought that Daniel could be actually be dead?

Daniel responded unto the king, "O KING! LIVE FOREVER! My God sent his angel, and he shut the mouths of the lions. They have not hurt me, because innoncency was found in me. Nor have I ever done any wrong before you, Your Majesty." The king was exceedingly glad for Daniel. He instructed that Daniel be taken out of the den; Daniel experienced no hurt because he absolutely believed in his God.

As you read the story of Daniel and his innocence, note the reaction of the king. He brought the men who had accused Daniel and cast them into the den of lions. The Bible says, "At the king's command, the men who had falsely accused Daniel were brought in and thrown into the lions' den, along with their wives and children. And before they reached the floor of the den, the hungry lions overpowered them and crushed all their bones."

The remarkable truth about Daniel is that God gave him dominion. Because of his favor, men trembled in fear before the God of Daniel. God is a living God who is steadfast forever. He delivered and rescued Daniel. He worketh signs and wonders in heaven and earth. So Daniel prospered.

When I was a little girl, my 3 sisters and I would visit down south in Alabama during the summer. Often, we would spend the summer with our grandparents. My grandfather was a faithful deacon in a church for forty years. He would start the prayer at the Rock Primitive Baptist Church at the beginning of service. I was amazed every time I saw my grandfather praying. He would go to the front bench at the church and bow down on one knee.

In my grandfather's case, kneeling was a sign of respect, reference, and a genuine awe of the Holy presence of God. While praying, I noticed when my grandfather would kneel, it seemed that he inspired a chorus of voices; individuals who would join in fervently in audible corporate prayer. With no music, the voices would ring in the sanctuary located in the red clay hills. There was a special level of anointing on the service as a result.

As a young girl who was extremely observant, I also noticed in the south a different level of respect with the people for one another. For instance, I noticed that every time there was a funeral procession, many people would pull their cars over to the side of the road, and some would step out of their cars, and I remember seeing men take off their hats and lower them, putting them to the side. They would bow their heads as a sign of respect as the family would pass by. Well, how much more should we bow our heads and understand that in prayer, it is a sign of respect and honor to our God, Yahweh, the Ancient of Days.

My Grandfather would say, "Lord, this is Your humble servant, and I come before You today with my knees bowed down. He would go on to say, "Thank you that I woke up this morning and my bed was not my cooling board." In essence, this prayer was a prayer of gratitude for another day and of life.

As we consider the gripping story of Daniel and the severity of the possible consequences he was facing for praying out loud through an open window, I am amazed at how God covered Daniel from harm and heard his petition. Despite the warning of the king, Daniel's persistence in praying three times a day kneeling gave indication of his bold tenacity.

I don't want anyone to take the posture of kneeling lightly. Although it is a common **posture of prayer**, it should be done with utmost intentionality, knowing this, that God will dispatch angels on your behalf. By faith the answer to your prayer shall come to pass.

It is recorded in the Book of *James, "it is the fervent, effectual prayers of the righteous man that availeth much." James 5:16* When you get on your knees to pray, I urge you not to be passive. It is my desire that you learn how to pray with fervency. The word fervent means to boil with intensity. It also indicates having or showing great enthusiasm as you are talking to God. I would like to give an example of our formative training in prayer.

There were times that I, along with my sisters, who are absolute treasures and powerful and anointed intercessors today, were in training. Our late mother and Pastor would strongly encourage us to pray from a place of passion. She taught us never to draw back during prayer. Her instructions included never be lukewarm but give your all while you are praying. Our mother said that we must pour out our hearts before the Lord.

In another instance, Dr. Angie Ray told me one morning when she was teaching us how to pray, "Come on Kim, it is your turn." As she would listen to the words our prayers expressed to God, she would teach us how we could improve by integrating the scripture into our communication, conversation, and daily dialogue with the Lord. Then mom would say to the next sister: "Tanya, it is your turn to pray." During that time, my baby sister Tanya was painfully shy but she developed her voice in prayer by talking aloud to God as we gathered together. Momma told her "Tanya, be bold, stop walking in fear." She explained that praying is communicating with the Lord; tap into the realm of the Spirit. I remember my mother sharing with my baby sister to pray to God like you're speaking to your best friend.

Mom would then say to my sister Cheryl, "it is your turn." Some days, Cheryl would ask mom, "Are you sure the Lord wants us to pray at 5:30 in the morning?" Her response was clear that she was still a bit sleepy. Cheryl obeyed and prayed with sincerity. There was a day that Cheryl heard about the death of our Pastor's father. After hearing this news, mom asked my sister Cheryl, "why are you weeping and crying?" Cheryl then responded, "how does it feel to lose your father?" Cheryl said "Elder Henton's father died and I feel hurt." Mom went on to explain to Cheryl what she was feeling was compassion in her heart. I believe that God was training her to be moved with compassion and concern for the plight of others and for humanity.

Not only did Cheryl have compassion, but my sister Denise also had a deep abiding sense of compassion and a tendency to pray merciful prayers of concern and to fight for the disadvantaged.

Mom would then turn to Denise and say, "It's your time your pray." Mom told Denise "Believe what you are praying for and trust that God will hear your prayers." Mom went on to teach, "After you have prayed to God, you must pray and war against the enemy." J. Denise Ray had an innate fight within her for the down trodden and for the mistreated; she would fight in the spirit on their behalf. Mom also told her, "End your prayers with a praise, knowing that you have victory by faith. "

When we would complete the prayer, Mom would give each of us bold, strong commentary, critique and sometimes rebuke. I remember her saying to me, "Kimberly, the next time you pray, I want you to forget about yourself, and I want you to call on the Lord with all of your strength." She instructed all of us,

"Never play games with God. If you're gonna pray, pray with purpose."

There were times she would say "And you can't be cute and into yourself while you're praying. You are not match for the devil in your flesh." Momma said, "You've got to call Him from your belly!" She taught us that out of your belly, rivers of living water would flow. She would say, "tap in." She taught us a sensitivity to the realm of the Spirit. One of the most important lessons that my mother taught me was never to let the Lord's presence go down. If the anointing was high in a service, she instructed us to keep the fire burning.

Are you a Prayer Warrior? I would like to echo some of the wisdom of my mother. Remember this when you're praying, we don't pray from a posture of weakness. But we pray with this in mind that the name of the Lord is a strong tower where the righteous run into it and they are safe. He is our Shield and our Buckler. (Psalm 94:4).

In times of battle, keep this in mind, God is a Battle-axe in the time of war. (Jeremiah 51:20). A battle-axe is God's destroying instrument. It was a mallet which is a heavy war club. This reference also includes a time of Spiritual battle, the Bible says for we wrestle not against flesh and blood but against spiritual wickedness in high places.

In Daniel chapter 10, Daniel is confronted by a demonic spirit that delayed, hindered and impeded him. As we look to Daniel's story, prayer is absolutely critical and crucial for spiritual warfare battles. Prayer will cause you to be alert in times of battle.

When the enemy comes after you, I implore you earnestly to get in the battle, and use the weapons of war. Apply and appropriate the blood of Jesus. Command every stronghold to break,

break, break! Keep in mind no weapon formed against you shall prosper. God has granted the power to bind and loose in prayer. Use the weapon in warfare.

In the book of Isaiah 41:10, the Bible declares "Fear thou not; for I am with thee: be not dismayed; for I am thy God: I will strengthen thee; yea, I will help thee; yea, I will uphold thee with the right hand of my righteousness." Ask God to arise. In Psalm 68:1, the Bible states "Let God arise, let his enemies be scattered."

I want you to understand if you are living a godly life and walking worthy of your vocation in holiness, you have the power to break the assignments of the enemy.

I want to assure you in times of prayer that the Lord of hosts, the God over earthy and heavenly armies, has given unto every believer power to bind and loose. You are seated in heavenly places, far above principalities.

According to the book of Matthew, Christians have been granted assistance from Heaven's armies in times of warfare. I encourage you to pray with this in mind. That the Lord of the armies is with you. The God of Jacob is your strong defense and fortress. Call upon the Lord and Almighty God will destroy, eradicate, and annihilate every demonic assignment over your life. Pray with this confidence that there is no match for our Almighty God.

"...to love mercy and to walk humbly with thy God."

-Micah 6:8b

Chapter 8
WALKING PRAYERS
"Take the Lord along with you everywhere you go"

MICAH

"...to love mercy and to walk humbly with thy God." Micah 6:8b

I remember sitting in a wonderful service as a God-fearing adolescent. I was listening very closely to the message that was given by a highly esteemed and beloved church mother. She was a respected Mother in Zion who was known for her fervent prayer life and for her love of the members of the congregation.

Before ministering, she sang a song that was so popular at our church. She lifted her voice with great power and boldly sang, "Take the Lord along with you everywhere you go, you're going to need him on your journey everywhere you go." This song stayed with me as it served as a reminder that you can pray on the go and be cognizant of God's presence at all times.

At times, she would have words after the song encouraging the members to always keep the Lord on their hearts and minds as you walk with Him daily. As I reflect on this exciting time in my life, I remember my time with Mother Pearline Nance as she would encourage us to walk Holy before God, daily. During this season, Mother Nance encouraged the saints to testify of their real-life situations. It is here where I learned the value and impact of a testimony. I was affected by the stories of the triumphant victories and trials. I was so moved that I asked to speak with Mother Nance once after hearing all of the saints testify week after week; I remember wanting to have my own testimony. I boldly proclaimed to Mother Nance, "Mother. I am ready for my trials and tribulations" so I could testify. She laughed vehemently and said "Kim, you don't have to ask for trials. Just keep living. But the Lord will see you through them all."

Though this was very funny, my sentiments at the time were real. I am so grateful for the insight I received from this woman of God. She urged us to keep the Lord as a frontlet before our eyes and to always pray as we go.

As a Pastor of over 18 years and having traveled as an Evangelist for over 39 years, the Lord has allowed me to be an personal eye witness to so many distinct testimonies. It is a high honor to pray. It is a beautiful opportunity to fellowship with our Majestic, Just, and respectfully August God. In my experience, I have found that there are many people who struggle with a sense of unspoken guilt regarding their prayer lives; many are discouraged and feel perpetually inadequate. This discouragement causes many to abandon seeking God and the attempt to pray altogether.

One of the things I've noticed in the lives of believer is an enormous amount of people who seem to carry a sense of guilt regarding their prayer lives. For example, so many say again and again, "I am too busy, I don't have time." As you read this chapter regarding the walking prayers, it is my hope that you recognize your ability and seize the opportunities to actually pray at all times.

In the book of Micah, the Lord revealed to the Prophet of God that he had a controversy with his people. Micah is a prophet in the Old Testament traditionally known as one of the 12 minor prophets. Micah's prophetic book contains sobering messages about justice, oppression, and judgment against corruption. It also details a prophesy about the future redemption and restoration of Israel. In the scripture, God reminded them that he had been faithful.

The Bible mentions that God said, "I brought you out of the house of Egypt" God says "Oh my people, what have I done unto thee and wherein have I wearied thee?" He then says "I have redeemed thee." Micah began to reason with God, offering a list of sacrifices that would satisfy Him. Micah the prophet asked the Lord, "Lord, how shall I come before you and bow myself before the high God?"

In this moment, Micah asked God the question in an earnest sense of urgency attempting to understand how he could please God, given the controversy. He asked the Lord, "Should I come before you with burnt offerings? Will it please you to bring thousands of rams of 10 thousand rivers of oil? Should I bring my first born, the fruit of my body for my transgressions or for the sin of my soul?" This is basically the answer.

In Micah 6:8, in this verse, it is a call to ethical living, embracing the importance of justice, mercy, and humility. The Bible says, "He hath shewed thee, O man, what is good; and what doth the LORD require of thee but to do justly, and to love mercy, and to walk humbly with thy God?" This is what the Lord wants from His people. It is not blood sacrifices that God is looking for. In the context of this scripture, he is expecting man to do justly. This is an indication that He is looking for righteousness and doing that which is upright in the sight of God. It is also very clear that the instruction is to love mercy.

The biblical meaning of the word "mercy" is more kindness than justice requires. When I speak of mercy, it is also described as also compassion and forgiveness shown towards someone whom it is within one's power to harm. It involves refraining from inflicting punishment upon someone who may actually deserve it. Showing mercy emanates from a sense of fairness, compassion, and loving kindness.

Another requirement that is requested is to "walk humbly with God." I want to include the story of Micah in the **postures of prayer** as we glean that God wants His people to humbly walk before Him. Walking humbly also includes one's relationship with God which has always been defined as a walk! For example, as we walk humbly before the Lord, it allows another **posture of prayer** which keeps an open dialogue with the Lord as you walk and talk with him daily.

As a young girl, I remember hearing a song that says, "Walk with me Lord, walk with me. While I'm on this tedious journey, I want you Lord, to walk with me."

As a believer, you are to walk humbly with God. For we walk by faith and not by sight. We are encouraged to walk in the Spirit and not in the flesh. While walking from one place to another, you can pray quietly, speaking to God about any subject. Prayer transcends time and space. It is an incredible joy to know that you can talk to God while walking to any location. This also speaks of having dependence upon God as you learn and grow. As you walk and pray, I encourage you to keep a humble attitude of meekness, gratitude, and respect to avoid all semblance of pride or arrogance.

Can I share something with you? To those of you who have this mindset, "Pastor Kim, I just don't have time to pray and here's why, because I am busy. I have children, I have a husband, I have a wife, I have a family, I have all of these responsibilities and I work." These are the reasons people give as to why they don't have time to pray. Well, I want you to be strengthened in your prayer life by adding this postures of prayer, the walking prayer.

A walking prayer is grasping available time to see God. It is when you're on your way to work, before you clock-in, for example, you can pray, "Father, in the name of Jesus, let the blood of Jesus Christ prevail. I appropriate the precious blood of Jesus over my family, my children and all who are connected to me. Lord, I honor you for your goodness and Your mercy towards me. Thank you for your love and for your redemption."

You don't have to wait to pray. But you can pray on your way to church, or on your way to school. You can pray on the go, at any moment, at any time. And not only that, there are those of you who are stay-at-home mothers that have to clean, and do chores such as washing, ironing, and vacuuming. I hope to inspire you to take opportunities to pray and communicate with our Sovereign God in those moments.

In the Bible, Luke 18:2 states that men ought always to pray and not faint. We glean from the book of Micah that we can walk and talk with God 24 hours a day in prayer.

Our Christian Walk has been defined as a race. Solomon said the race is not to the swift nor the battle to the strong. In conclusion, I remind you of the words of Isaiah *"but they that wait upon the Lord shall renew their strength; they shall mount up on wings as eagles; they shall run and not be weary, **and they shall walk,** and not faint."* Isaiah 40:31

"And she was a widow of about fourscore and four years, which departed not from the temple, but served God with fastings and prayers night and day."

-Luke 2:37

Chapter 9

Prayers in the Temple

"Let the church say amen"

ANNA

"And she was a widow of about fourscore and four years, which departed not from the temple, but served God with fastings and prayers night and day." Luke 2:37

*I*n the book of Luke, there was a woman in the Bible by the name of Anna. Her name means "favor or grace." There are only three verses found in the New Testament book of Luke concerning Anna. Anna was a prophetess unto the Lord of the tribe of Asher who lived in Jerusalem during the time of Jesus' birth. She was known as spiritually virtuous. Asher is significant in the Bible as it was one of the original twelve tribes of Israel. Traditionally, the women of the tribe of Asher were remarkable for their beauty and talent. The women of the tribe of Asher were noted as being so beautiful that Priests and Princes sought after them. This tribe was also known for their abundance of oil. The soil was fertile in times of scarcity.

The Bible says that Moses stated of Asher that it would be the most blessed of the sons of Jacob and favored of its descendants. Before Jacob, who was the father of the tribes, died, he blessed his sons. During the blessing, Jacob said, "Asher's food would be rich and fit for a king."

Anna was of great age; she was eighty-four and had lived with her husband for seven years until his death. She became a widow and made a decision to depart not from the temple. Anna is recorded in scripture as one who served God with fasting and prayer, night and day. As Anna sought the Lord, she gave thanks unto Him and prayed for all who looked for the redemption of Jerusalem. She was waiting in the temple to see the coming of the promised Messiah.

The day came that Anna was with Mary and Joseph and she began praising God. She talked about the child to everyone who had been waiting expectantly for the redemption of Jerusalem.

When Anna sees the infant Jesus in the temple, she immediately recognizes Him as the long-awaited Lord and Savior. She had the privilege of witnessing a fact unprecedented throughout history. She began honoring and thanking God for allowing her to see Him with her own eyes, the awaited hope of her people.

Anna's story reminds me of the word "amen." The basic meaning of the word amen is firm, fixed, or sure. The related Hebrew verb "amen" also means to be reliable and to be trusted. The Old Testament usually translates amen as "so be it." It is also frequently described as "verily" or "truly."

Anna had a blessed assurance that her eyes were beholding the promised Messiah and King. Can you imagine what she must have said, knowing the fulfillment of a century's old prophecy? This term "amen" came to mind and is often used in churches all over the world. It is an indicator that individuals in the church are in agreement with what they have heard.

Luke 2:38 states "Anna was present as Simeon was talking with Mary and Joseph, and she began praising God. She talked about the child to everyone who had been waiting expectantly for God to rescue Jerusalem." They made a purification offering and presented Jesus as their first born unto God.

Simeon was a righteous and devout man of God who was also eagerly awaiting the Messiah. The Holy Spirit was upon him and revealed to him that he would not die until he had seen the Lord's Messiah. On this particular day, the Spirit led him to the Temple. When Mary and Joseph came to present Jesus, Simeon was there. He praises God and utters a prophecy concerning Jesus and Mary. It is recorded that Simeon cradles the Lord Jesus in his arms.

We see that Anna's life is indeed overflowing with favor and grace that was spoken of her lineage in the Old Testament. Anna is among a few precious Biblical women who embraced the sacred title of Prophetess; she freely dedicated herself to the temple and as a vessel Holy unto the Lord. It is inspiring to observe the life of Anna who spent her days worshiping the Lord, fasting day and night, and praying faithfully in the temple.

Lastly, her many years of sacrifice and service were worth it all, as she had the blessed honor of beholding the Messiah, the Lord Jesus Christ, whom she longed for years to see.

Anna shares the good news with everyone that she encountered; that the Redeemer had come and the age-old prophecies were being fulfilled. Imagine, Anna was one of the first very eyewitnesses of the Savior of the world. This was the answer to Anna's posture of fasting and praying in the temple, an actual fulfillment of a promise from God. Let the church say amen!

"He lifted His eyes towards heaven to pray."

-St. John 11:41

Chapter 10

LIFTING EYES IN PRAYER

"Father, I know that you always hear me"

JESUS

"He lifted His eyes towards heaven to pray."
St. John 11:41

What I love about prayer is that it is a beautiful opportunity to share communication between God and man. Corporate prayer creates a setting of unity and strengthens the bond of fellowship. Yes, we can pray kneeling, standing, bowing our heads and in this case, like Jesus, we can pray looking up toward heaven.

As a teenager, I recall seeing one of my uncles who was a Pastor of a church in Chicago. His voice was so powerful; he would state "the doors of the church are open." This was an invitation extended to the congregation at the close of the Sunday sermon where worshippers are welcome to publicly come forward to accept Jesus Christ as Lord.

Jesus prayed exhibiting unshakeable and unwavering faith. As we observe His dialogue with the Father, I was struck by Jesus' ability to speak to God with incredible assurance. We can follow His example when we pray by praying from a place of absolute confidence.

A word of caution: our goal is not to pray to be seen by man; we are not to pray as an outward act nor a show like those of false religious piety. We can clearly glean from Jesus Christ in His times of prayer that He was moved with compassion for humanity. There are even times when we pray in secret, in our prayer closet, and watch God reward the petition openly.

In the book of John, *"These words spake Jesus, and lifted up his eyes to heaven, and said, Father, the hour is come; glorify thy Son, that thy Son also may glorify thee"* John 17:1.

The disciple John, who is described as the disciple whom Jesus loved, writes a moving narrative about Jesus Christ. John describes the account of Jesus Christ as He returned from a time away. During the time Jesus was away on his journey, Lazarus died. Lazarus was the brother of Mary and her sister Martha of the town of Bethany, a village on the southeastern slope on the Mount of Olives about two miles east of Jerusalem. Bethany was a beautiful village known for its tranquility and peace.

This is the Mary which anointed the Lord Jesus with ointment. She and her sister were devastated because their brother Lazarus died. Jesus was on his way to them however, He abode there two extra days. The purpose of this delay was to cause unbelievers who were following him to believe.

Jesus returned and found that Lazarus had been in the grave for four days. Many people came to comfort Mary and Martha concerning their brother. Martha said to the Lord, "If thou hast been here, my brother had not died." It was clear that she was in the state of displeasure, sadness, and devastating disappointment. She was in a place where her hopes and expectations were dashed. The scripture states in the Old testament that hope deferred makes the heart sick.

I am amazed at how she said to Jesus "I know even now whatsoever thou will ask of God; God will give it to thee." During this conversation, Jesus said unto her, "Thy brother shall rise again." Martha said unto him, "I know that He shall rise again in the resurrection at the last day."

As I share the words of this scripture with you today, I would like to ask you to take note of this. Jesus responded to Martha saying emphatically, "I am the resurrection and the life. He that believeth in me, though he were dead, yet shall he live." Martha re-establishes in this moment her faith in Him by saying, "Ye Lord, I believe that thou art the Christ the Son of God which shall come into the world."

I would like to ask you to closely observe how Jesus walked in the midst of people who were watching every word that he spoke and observing every move that He made. In this account, Mary and Martha were weeping but Jesus groaned in the Spirit and was troubled. His question to them was, "Where have you laid him?" I love their response: "Lord, come and see."

It must have been daunting for Jesus to hear the people standing around saying "Could not this man which opened the eyes of the blind have prevented the death of Lazarus?"

Jesus, deeply moved and therefore groaning in Himself, came to the grave. The scripture describes it as a cave and the stone lay upon it. Jesus said "take ye away the stone." In this moment, Martha said to Jesus "Lord, by this time he stinketh for he hath been dead four days." According to tradition, the dead body was not truly or completely considered dead until the fourth day. It was upon the fourth day that the body starts the process of the final stages of decomposition and rigor mortis.

Jesus said unto her, "If thou would believe, thou shall see the glory of God." They took away the stone from the place where Lazarus was laying.

Herein is the posture of Jesus. In prayer, Jesus lifted His eyes to heaven and said, "Father, I thank thee that thou hast heard me". According to the book of Matthew, the eyes are the lamp of the body. The eyes are also described as the window to the soul. Jesus lifted His eyes to His Father with absolute confidence as He prayed for the healing of Lazarus. I believe that it is wonderful to allow hope in God to inspire you to lift your eyes in prayer. It is a sign of absolute confidence in God's ability to answer your prayers.

I would like to ask you to notice this powerful fact. During this posture of prayer, Jesus looked up toward heaven, speaking directly to His Heavenly Father with bold confidence and assurance. In the face of His opposition, those who did not believe, and individuals who discounted His ability to help Lazarus, Jesus spoke to His Father, looking up toward heaven, thanking Him that He always hears Him when He prays.

Why look up to heaven? It implies a type of reassurance that God stands with Jesus in prayer, His words, and His actions. Jesus looks towards heaven in a moment of confident fortitude knowing that God has heard Him.

Heaven is described primarily as God's dwelling place in the Biblical tradition. I believe it is noteworthy to distinguish the word heaven. The word heaven in Hebrew meaning is (Shamayim) and in the Greek, the word (Ouranos) which are both translated as the word sky. It is a canvas for the Divine. Heaven is where God manifests His power, communicates

His promises, and displays His eternal glory.

This is noted as a realm where everything operates according to God's will. Heaven is known as God's dwelling place in the Bible. It is also referred to as paradise known for being immaculate and indescribably beautiful. Heaven inspires faith in God and hope for eternity.

There were times Jesus prayed within himself, not always speaking aloud. It is clear that at some juncture along the journey, Jesus prayed for the healing of Lazarus within Himself, because in this moment, He was offering thanksgiving that God had already heard Him. I absolutely love the fact that Jesus had such a unified bond with God, His Father.

He acknowledged His Father in prayer and spoke words of thanks to God for not just hearing Him in that moment, but that He hears him every time He prays.

Now Jesus prays aloud so that the people standing by may hear. He said, "I know that thou hearest me always but for the benefit of the people which standby," Jesus said, "that they might believe that thou has sent me."

In the next moment, Jesus cried with authority in a loud voice, "Lazarus! Come forth!" The crowd around the tomb were standing in a place of doubt. As this dead man slowly hobbled out of the cave. The crowd around the tomb were now in a state of awe, shock, and utter dismay. Lazarus was still bound with burial clothes; this is of great significance. Grave clothes were strips of white linen cloth used to wrap the body with various spices to cover some of the strong odor of a decaying body in the grave. Lazarus' face was bond with a napkin which was a large handkerchief. Jesus said, "Loose him and let him go!" Lazarus was healed and the people gave glory to God. This miracle increased the faith of Jesus' followers just as Jesus said it would.

There is another instance in the scripture I'd like for you to observe. This story occurs in the garden of Gethsemane at a time when Jesus went away to pray. He took Peter with Him and the two sons of Zebedee. This was a very heavy moment. The Bible describes that Jesus said "My soul is exceeding sorrowful even unto death. Tarry ye here and watch with me." During this passionate prayer, Jesus came face to face with the reality that He must pay the cost for the sins of mankind. In a moment of humanity, He said, "Oh my Father, if it be possible, let this cup pass from me. Nevertheless, not as I will but as thou will."

Jesus Christ is our perfect example. I believe that in times of distress, having done all that you can to do what is right, sometimes it requires moments of submission and surrender to the divine will of God. There is something extraordinary about the wrestle of the human will and the will of God. At times it can be a very intense war. It takes humility and trust to pray fervently on one's face in an effort to seek the heart of God, only for His perfect will.

Jesus prayed the prayer twice, "Oh Father, let this cup pass from me." In the second instance, He had come to His disciples and found them asleep. He asked this question, "What, could ye not watch with me one hour?" There are times in prayer when others around you may not sense the gravity of your concern. It can be disappointing to expect others to pray during those daunting times. I encourage you to lay out before God, pour out your heart and soul before Him in prayer. May I assure you that God knows and He will answer your cry.

I have to share another instance where Jesus displayed a posture of prayer by looking up to heaven. In Matthew 14:19, the Bible says, "And he directed the people to sit down on the grass. Taking the five loaves and the two fish and looking up to heaven, he gave thanks and broke the loaves."

In this verse, as Jesus is teaching the crowd about relying on God for substance, He directed the people to sit down. Jesus acknowledged the presence of His Father. By looking up to heaven, he exemplifies this truth, that God is the source of miracles. He also indicates that provision came from God and not merely human effort. I believe that Jesus looked to His Father as a gesture of His dependence on Him.

Let this example be a source of inspiration in times in which circumstances seem insurmountable. I pray that you will glean from this prayer the courage to look up, despite the obstacles, and know that your Heavenly Father has the power to provide. The Lord will make a way for you.

"Therefore, I want the men everywhere to pray, lifting up holy hands without anger or disputing."

-1st Timothy 2:8 (NIV)

Chapter 11

LIFTING HOLY HANDS IN PRAYER

"Everybody Lift Your Hands"

Paul the Apostle

Therefore I want the men everywhere to pray, lifting up holy hands without anger or disputing. 1st Timothy 2:8 (NIV)

*I*f anyone should ask me who is one of my favorite Biblical vessels in the New Testament, I would say the Apostle Paul. Arguably, he is one of the most important figures in the New Testament writings. As I have studied many of his letters, I am most moved by this stark reality that some of his letters were written from prison. He had an uncanny way of encouraging the churches to remain steadfast and follow after the teachings of the Lord Jesus Christ.

In this moment, I focus the next posture of prayer on Apostle Paul. In general, he is regarded as one of the most important figures of the Apostolic Age. Paul the apostle says, "That I may know him, and the power of his resurrection, and the fellowship of his suffering, being made conformable unto his death." Philippians 3:10

Paul was an advocate of the scriptures. His teacher was Gamaliel who was noted as one of the greatest teachers. In 1st Timothy 2, Paul gives guidelines for the church. He says, "I exhort therefore, that, first of all, supplications, prayers, intercessions, and giving of thanks, be made for all men, for kings, and for all that are in authority; that we may lead a quiet and peaceable life in all godliness and honesty."

Paul goes on to establish "For this is good and acceptable in the sight of God our Savior." Paul was an advocate addressing various aspects of prayer and leadership within the church. I love how he instructs everyone including authority to pray. He places special emphasis on this truth; that it is possible to live a quiet and peaceable life, free from constant conflict.

In this chapter, Paul admonishes them to be saved and come into the knowledge of the truth. He goes on to explain that there is one God, one mediator between God and man, the man Christ Jesus explaining that Jesus gave Himself a ransom for all. For this purpose, Paul states that I am ordained a "preacher and an apostle."

In Christianity, an Apostle refers to a person who has been chosen by the Lord to spread His teachings and to establish His church. The term "Apostle" comes from the Greek word "Apostolos", which means one who is sent out on a mission for the purpose of spreading His teachings and establishing His church. Paul states, "I speak the truth in Christ and lie not. I am a teacher in faith and truth."

The scripture goes on to say that Paul the Apostle Paul gave special instructions. He said "I will therefore that men pray everywhere, lifting up holy hands without wrath or doubting." In this text, Paul gives specific instructions on how to pray. He suggests that men everywhere pray, lifting Holy hands. The phrase Holy hands is mentioned in the context of prayer. It is a metaphorical expression signifying sincerity, purity, and divine reverence as we pray.

As a teacher, the Apostle Paul exhorts his own son in the faith, Timothy, that men should never pray to a Holy God from a position of hostility, wrath, anger, resentment, or contentiousness. He warned against praying in doubt which is described as a feeling of uncertainty or lack of conviction. One of the reasons that Paul instructed them not to have doubt is because of this truth: faith moves God. Without faith, it is impossible to please the Lord. Doubt has an insidious way of tearing down hopeful expectations and smothers a believer's outlooks.

In the Bible, James describes what doubt will do to a man. He states a double minded man is unstable in all of his ways. James goes on to say that a man who doubts is like "a wave of the sea that is driven and tossed by the wind." James 1:6

There is a biblical example where Jesus asks Peter, "Why did you doubt?" Peter was walking on the water toward Jesus. He began to look around and notice the waves of the sea and the tumultuous winds. It is when Peter took his eyes off Jesus that he began to doubt and sink. Thus saying to Jesus in this moment of terror, one of the shortest prayers in the Bible, "Lord, save me!" It is my hope to provide information to glean from to apply to your walk with God and help you if you are struggling in the area of doubt.

Doubt will block your prayers because it opposes the faith that is required to please God. The next time you're in a church service and the request is made for you to lift your hands, think of Paul and his instruction to "lift your hands with sincerity, without resentment, anger, bitterness or doubt in your mind." Cast down every thought of doubt, fear, or unbelief and make a concerted effort with everything in you to bless the Lord with all of your might and strength.

Today, I hope that you see prayer in a fresh new light. The next time you read the Apostle Paul's letter which states "pray without ceasing," in 1st

Thessalonians 5:17, that this **posture of prayer** comes to mind.

Prayer is a conversation from your heart, speaking your authentic truth to God. It is a fellowship between a gracious God and mankind.

"Lift up your hands in the sanctuary, and bless the Lord."

-Psalm 134:2

Closing Prayer

Lord, how great is Your goodness and how great is Your beauty. Thank you for your power to hear the faintest cry and our whisper. Father, in the name of Jesus, I pray for every person who's eyes fall upon this prayer. Allow them to search for You and find your original path and perfect will designated for their lives. I ask that you will place a hunger and thirst to know who You are…Your voice, Your strength, and Your ways. I ask you now to give them fortitude and determination to live a life that is pleasing unto you. Help them to walk worthy of Your vocation. Give them the ability to retain the information shared in this book, The Postures of Prayer. Help them to discover why prayers were answered and solutions were given in the scripture. Lord, I come to You and I ask you to grant my request. Give this reader a life-changing experience in You. Strengthen them with wisdom and knowledge. Lord, you are the God of hope, now fill your people with abundant joy and peace in believing that in You, they abound in hope through the power of the Holy Ghost. Lord, surround Your people with healing love. May the Postures of Prayer remain as a part of the daily prayer lives of Your people. For thine is the kingdom, and the power, and the glory both now and forever. **Amen.**

A letter of love from the author

Writing a book about the postures of prayer has been one of my greatest joys. It is my soul's desire that your personal relationship with our Eternal God will be strengthened by the information that has been provided and that you experience a greater capacity to pray with a new insight. My final prayer for you is that you embrace the postures of prayer as opportunities to remain cognizant and aware of God's presence as you go through your daily life. I encourage you to keep joyfully pressing on in fervent prayer until the will of God for your life is revealed. Honor the Lord and continue praying until you have become what He has intended for you to be. Remember that you were born with a purpose and placed in the earth to glorify God and to be a vessel for His use.

May the weight of the glory of the
Lord and His fresh anointing that
destroys yokes continuously rest upon
you.

All my love,

Pastor Kimberly L. Ray

*"The spirit of prayer is essentially the
spirit of love. Intercession is simply love
at work."*

The Lord's Prayer

Our Father which art in heaven,
Hallowed be thy name.
Thy kingdom come,
Thy will be done in earth, as it is in
heaven.
Give us this day our daily bread.
And forgive us our debts, as we
forgive our debtors.
And lead us not into temptation,
but deliver us from evil:
For thine is the kingdom, and the
power, and the glory, for ever.
Amen.

-Matthew 6:9-13

"I will lift up mine eyes unto the hills, from whence cometh my help."

-Psalm 121:1

"Confess your faults one to another, and pray one for another, that ye may be healed. The effectual fervent prayer of a righteous man availeth much."

-James 5:16

Made in the USA
Columbia, SC
27 August 2024